MATHNET™ CASEBOOK

#1 The Case of The Unnatural

By David D. Connell and Jim Thurman

Illustrated by Danny O'Leary

Scientific
BOOKS FOR YOUNG READERS
American

Children's Television Workshop

W. H. Freeman/New York

Printed in the United States of America

Scientific American Books for Young Readers is an imprint of W.H. Freeman
and Company, 41 Madison Avenue, New York, New York 10010

On Mathnet, the role of George Frankly is played by Joe Howard; the role of
Pat Tuesday is played by Toni Di Buono; the role of Benny Pill is played by
Barry K. Willerford; the role of Captain Joe Grecco is played by Emilio Del
Pozo. The role of Casey Bengal is played by Paul Dooley.

Cover photo of Joe Howard, Toni Di Buono, and Paul Dooley
© CTW/Richard Termine

Illustrated by Danny O'Leary

Activities by Richard Dyches

Activity illustrations by Lynn Brunelle

Library of Congress Cataloging Number 93-18352

ISBN 0-7167-6506-3 (hardcover)
    0-7167-6504-7 (paper)

Second printing 1997, KP

CHAPTER

1

One crisp fall Monday morning, Pat Tuesday arrived at Mathnet HQ a bit late. She was about to open the door of the office when she heard an argument going on inside. She recognized the voices and smiled.

"You can too."

"You can not."

"Can too."

"Can not."

Pat opened the door and watched for a minute as her partner, George Frankly, and Benny Pill, an undercover cop, continued their debate. As she sat down at her desk, Pat said, "I love to hear intellectual debates between two heavyweight thinkers."

"Oh, good morning, Pat," said Benny cheerily. "George and I were just discussing slugging averages."

"I'm glad I got here before the violence began," said Pat.

She flipped through her phone messages while George explained. "We were debating baseball stats. I was just saying that even though a player's slugging average can be higher than his or her batting average, it is unlikely to be *four times* as high."

With a twinkle in her eye, Pat responded, "You wouldn't kid a partner, would you, George?"

"Never. See, batting averages show how many times a player gets a hit, but a slugging average tells you how many bases the player's gotten." George grabbed a yellow pad and began demonstrating how to calculate batting averages. "If a batter has been up 10 times, and gets 4 hits, you divide the number of hits by the times at bat. So 4 divided by 10—"

$$\frac{\text{\# of hits} = 4}{\text{times at bat} = 10}$$

"Point four," Pat said.

George pointed to the pad. "Actually, it's .400. In baseball we carry out the division to 3 figures."

"To the nearest thousandth," Benny added. "So we say this guy is hitting 400."

Pat asked, "Why not say 4/10 or .4 or 40 percent— he gets a hit 40 percent of the time?"

"Because in baseball, most batters get a hit every 3 or 4 times they are up," said George. "Players' averages would be too similar. By going to the thousandth point, we can see who is hitting just a bit more. For example, we can see that someone hitting .201 is hitting an average of about 2 out of 10 pitches. Someone hitting .299 is averaging 3 out of 10. If you just said .2, you couldn't tell the difference.

Pat nodded. "Then what was the argument?"

Benny and George used the yellow pad again to demonstrate how to work out a player's slugging average. This time they divided the total number of bases the player got by the times at bat.

total # of bases ÷ times at bat

4 singles ÷ 10 times at bat

$$\frac{4}{10} \qquad 10\overline{)4.00}\;\; .400$$

"So if the 4 hits our player got were each singles, that's a slugging average of 4 divided by 10, or, the same as the batting average," said Benny.

"I see," said Pat. "But suppose the 4 hits weren't just singles?"

George picked up the pad again. "Good question. Suppose the hits were all home runs. You get 4 bases for each home run, so that would be a total of 16 bases. The player's slugging average would be 16 divided by 10—1.6. Move the decimal three places and it's 1600."

$$10\overline{)16.00}\;\; 1.600$$

"Pretty impressive," Pat said. "Does anybody ever do that?"

"Roy 'Lefty' Cobbs does," Benny answered.

"I'm telling you, it's almost impossible," said George.

"Who's Roy 'Lefty' Cobbs?" Pat asked.

"He's an over-the-hill pitcher on a hot streak," Benny said. "He plays for a minor league club called the River Vale Rowdies. Lefty played in the majors but never really made it big, and for the last few years he's been bouncing around the minors."

"But this season he's been remarkable," George interrupted. "Lefty has won 13 straight games pitching and is hitting .718. That's amazing even for the minor leagues. In those 13 games, he's been at bat 39 times and gotten 28 hits!"

Benny told Pat, "If the streak continues, every major league team will try to sign Lefty for next season. He's the talk of the baseball world!"

Benny looked at his watch. "It's almost 10 o'clock. Gotta run. Thanks for the slugging lesson, George."

George smiled. "Anytime, Mr. P., anytime."

The baseball debate over, Pat began opening the mail on her desk. "George, listen to this."

Dear Mathnetters,

I am worried about a dear friend and I think you can help me. I would like to meet with you on Monday at 10 A.M.

Sincerely,
Babs Bengal

George said, "I wonder what that's all about."

The intercom buzzed.

"Tuesday," Pat answered. "Oh hi, Sergeant Abruzzi.

Fine, send her up." Pat hung up and looked at her partner. "George, we'll soon find out. Babs Bengal is here."

* * *

The Mathnet HQ door opened and a 12-year-old girl poked her head in. She had freckles, a sandy-colored ponytail, and a worried expression.

"Babs Bengal?" Pat inquired. Babs nodded.

"I'm Pat Tuesday, and this is my partner, George—"

"Frankly, Mathnet," George finished, smiling at Babs.

"Sit down, Babs. What can we do for you?" Pat asked.

Babs sat on the edge of a chair and looked the Mathnetters over. "I need you to help me with a dear friend."

"Is your friend sick or something?" George asked.

"Yes . . . well, I mean no. I mean, well, maybe he's sick or—"

Pat gently interrupted. "Why do you think your friend needs help?"

"Because his number sequencing doesn't make sense any more," she blurted out.

"His number sequencing?" George asked.

"Normally, I can figure them out. But lately, he's been all over the map," said Babs. "See, we play this game. One of us starts a number sequence—"

"Number sequence? Like 2-4-6-8?"

"Right, Ms. Tuesday. The other person has to guess the next four numbers in the sequence. In this case, 10-12-14-16."

"But Babs, the next four numbers could be any four numbers at all."

"Of course they *could,* Mr. Frankly. But the game is, I have to guess the next four numbers in his sequence. We call it 'Guess My Rule.'" She pointed to the blackboard next to the computer. "May I show you?"

She picked up the chalk and began scribbling numbers on the board.

"He writes his numbers, let's say 1-3-7-15, on the outside of a sealed envelope. Inside the envelope is a sheet with the answer, the next four numbers in his sequence. I have to try to guess what rule he's using and what those next four numbers will be."

George took the chalk and wrote as he spoke. "I get it. The next four numbers might be 31-63-127-255."

Babs smiled. "Exactly. So I make my guess, write it down, then open the envelope and see if I'm right. If I am, I win and I get to make up the next sequence. If I'm wrong, he goes again. How did you figure that one out, Mr. Frankly?"

"I think the rule is double each number and then add 1. See, 1 doubled is 2. Add 1 more, it's 3. Then 3

$1 \times 2 = 2$	$2 + 1 = 3$
$3 \times 2 = 6$	$6 + 1 = 7$
$7 \times 2 = 14$	$14 + 1 = 15$
$15 \times 2 = 30$	$30 + 1 = 31$
$31 \times 2 = 62$	$62 + 1 = 63$
$63 \times 2 = 126$	$126 + 1 = 127$
$127 \times 2 = 254$	$254 + 1 = 255$

doubled is 6. Add 1, it's 7. Finally, 7 doubled is 14. Add 1, it's 15," George answered.

Babs frowned, then nodded. "That's good, but the way I got it was by looking at the differences between the pairs of numbers. The difference between 1 and 3 is 2, between 3 and 7 is 4, between 7 and 15 is 8. See? 2-4-8." She wrote on the board as she was explaining.

$$3 - 1 = \textcircled{2}$$
$$7 - 3 = \textcircled{4}$$
$$15 - 7 = \textcircled{8}$$

2×2
4×2

"Each difference is double the difference before. So if the rule holds," Babs continued, "the next difference will be 16, or 2 times 8. So I added 16 to the last number, 15, and got 31, the next number in the sequence."

"Two different solutions to the same problem," Pat said. "Pretty good game. So what's the problem?"

"The problem is that about a month ago my opponent flipped out. I can't make any sense out of his patterns anymore."

"But, as George said, a number sequence can go anywhere. The choices are infinite."

"True, Ms. Tuesday, but my friend and I have a rule. The numbers have to get bigger. That means no number can be repeated."

Pat nodded. "That's an arbitrary rule, but as long as

you both agree, no problem."

"We did agree," Babs said. "But look at this sequence." Babs erased the first sequence from the board and wrote another.

$$1 - 5 - 10 - 16$$

George and Pat pondered the numbers.

"I think I get it," Pat said. "He added 4 to the first number, 5 to the second, and 6 to the third." She took the chalk and began writing. "So you add 7 to the fourth number, that's 23. Add 8 to the fifth number, that's 31. Add 9 to the sixth number, that's 40. Add 10 to the seventh, and that's 50."

$$1-5-10-16$$

$$1+4 = \boxed{5}$$
$$5+5 = \boxed{10}$$
$$10+6 = \boxed{16}$$
$$16+7 = \boxed{23}$$
$$23+8 = \boxed{31}$$
$$31+9 = \boxed{40}$$
$$40+10 = \boxed{50}$$

"The answer would be 23-31-40-50," Pat concluded.

"Exactly what I thought," said Babs, writing the numbers on the board. "But his answer was 3-1-16-20-9-22-5. It breaks the rule."

"Maybe your opponent had a mental lapse on that

particular sequence," Pat suggested.

"That was only one example, Ms. Tuesday. He gave me this one today." She added the new sequence to the board.

$$1 - 4 - 10 - 22$$

George studied the numbers. "I see a possible sequence."

He wrote:

$$\textcircled{1} + 1 = 2 \qquad 2 \times 2 = \textcircled{4}$$
$$1 + 4 = 5 \qquad 5 \times 2 = \textcircled{10}$$
$$1 + 10 = 11 \qquad 11 \times 2 = \textcircled{22}$$

"See the pattern?" said George. "I added 1 and doubled the number. The answer would be 46-94-190-382."

Babs took a slip of paper out of her pocket and shoved it at them. "That's what I did, too. But look what he sealed up for his answer." This time, the sequence she copied out was longer.

$$11 - 9 - 4 - 14 - 1 - 16 - 16 - 5 - 4 - 313 - 23 - 98 - 114 - 10025$$

"It breaks the ground rule again."

"Right, Pat," said George. "The numbers get bigger

and smaller, and they repeat."

"Do you see why I'm worried?" Babs asked.

"Yes, I'd be a little concerned," said Pat. "Have you talked to him?"

Babs shook her head. "Not much. He doesn't seem to have time for me anymore."

George asked, "Has he been sick or anything like that lately?"

"He had a bad case of the flu a while ago and was out for a few days, but that's it. I guess he has been under a little pressure lately," Babs admitted. "Maybe that's all it is."

"What does he do for a living?" George asked. "Some stressful job maybe, like stockbroker, airline pilot, or Doberman pinscher trainer?"

"Oh, no. Nothing like that. He's a baseball player."

"A baseball player? What team is he on?" asked Pat.

"The River Vale Rowdies."

George and Pat looked at each other, then at Babs. "What's his name?"

"Roy 'Lefty' Cobbs."

DUM DE DUM DUM

CHAPTER

2

Tuesday dawned sunny and cool. Pat and George enjoyed the clear skies and autumn colors as they drove out of the city and into the lush Pascack Valley of northern New Jersey. Babs had invited them to watch the River Vale Rowdies practice that morning. That way, they could get a firsthand look at her friend Lefty.

George parked the car near the main entrance of the stadium and made their way to the bleachers inside. The Rowdies were spread all over the field, some playing "pepper," some batting, some catching "fungos" in the outfield. A few players were just stretching, jogging, and playing catch. The air was filled with the sounds of hickory on cowhide and the thunk of baseballs being snagged by leather gloves.

The Mathnetters were taking it all in, when George spotted Babs. She was in uniform and wearing a baseball glove.

"Pat, look. It's Babs. What's she doing?" George waved. Babs trotted over to where they were seated.

"Hi, Mathnetters. Thanks for coming."

"Babs, you didn't tell us you were on the team," said Pat.

"Well, I'm not exactly *on* it. I'm the ballgirl."

George nodded. "You're the one down the line who picks up foul balls and such?"

"That's right, Mr. Frankly."

George mused. "Boy, what a job. I wish I had been a ballgirl when I was a little boy."

"Excuse me?" said Babs. Pat just gave George a look and asked, "How long have you been doing this, Babs?"

"Three years, but I've got an in. My grandfather is the manager of the team."

George perked up. "Your grandfather is Casey Bengal?"

Babs pointed. "Yep. There he is."

George and Pat zeroed in on a man with graying hair. He had a belly that hung over his belt, but he moved gracefully, and he was clearly in command of everything happening on the practice field. He seemed to be calling out instructions to all of the 25 or 30 players at once.

"Pat, Casey Bengal is one of the real characters in the history of the game."

Pat nodded. "The name does sound vaguely familiar."

"He's *that* all right."

"What, Babs?"

"Vague. He's been like that as long as I can remember."

George turned to Pat and began speaking in one long, wandering sentence with no pauses. "I hear he talks in a one-long-sentence kind of way that sometimes doesn't make a lot of sense unless you think about it and then it kind of does or anyway so I hear." George stopped and took a deep breath.

Babs laughed. "That's a pretty good imitation, Mr. Frankly. Would you like to meet him?"

"Would I!"

Babs led George and Pat through a small maze of bats, balls, and players and over to Casey.

"Gramps, meet my friends Pat Tuesday and George Frankly. They're from Mathnet."

Casey looked at them. "Nice to meet you all around and welcome to the home field where we play at."

George shook Casey's hand. "It's a great honor to meet you, sir."

Pat added, "And congratulations on your successful season."

Casey lightly doffed his cap to Pat. "Thanks for saying that to me because it's wonderful so far unless something goes wrong which it always can only I hope it doesn't."

"Is Lefty Cobbs practicing today, Casey?" asked George.

Casey looked puzzled.

"Number 13, Gramps." Babs jumped in. "He calls all the players by their numbers," she explained.

"Number 13 should be out any time now unless he's later than that," said Casey.

"Number 13 is sure on a hot streak, isn't he, Casey?" Pat asked.

"Oh yes. Of course hot streaks have a way of cooling off you know averaging out over the long haul because nobody can keep doing what 13 is doing for a whole lifetime."

Babs said, "We just hope he stays hot until we

clinch the flag."

"Yes or win the pennant and go on to the minor league World Series," Casey agreed.

"I heard a rumor that if you win the pennant, you might get a chance to manage in the big leagues next year," said George.

"That's what they tell me and what I tell them is I'd love that chance and would give almost anything but my shoes for it but not my shoes because of the harsh winters where I live off season."

As Casey spoke, two men emerged from the dugout. One wore a baseball uniform; The other wore a loud plaid sports coat, houndstooth slacks, and a straw hat. "Hey, guys! There's Lefty," said Babs, the first to notice the odd pair.

"Who's that fellow with him? The guy talking on the mobile phone?" George asked.

"That's his jerky trainer and agent, Dr. Frank N. Steenbrenner."

Pat was surprised by Bab's sudden anger. "You don't like him?"

"No way. He's with Lefty all the time and hardly lets us talk."

Casey shrugged. "But he trains 13 good and rubs ointments on him and gives him special exercises and ices his elbow between innings and in general has done good for him somehow even though what's good for the pitcher is not always good for the gander. Or the first baseman."

George watched Steenbrenner and Lefty. "How long has he been with Lefty?" he asked Babs.

"Steenbrenner's the doctor Lefty went to when he

had the flu, and they've been together ever since. That's when Lefty changed. He's been acting funny. Watch."

Babs ran over to Lefty, who was popping a ball in his glove. She waited for him to notice her, but he didn't.

"Hi, Lefty. Did you do a number sequence for me today?"

Lefty gave Babs an empty look, as though he didn't recognize her. Then he said, "Isn't it a great day for a baseball game? Let's play a twin bill."

Suddenly, Frank N. Steenbrenner charged over to Babs and Lefty. "Listen, little girl, I've told you to keep away from Lefty," he growled. "He's got to concentrate on the game. Now beat it!" He led Lefty away across the field.

"You'd better get with it, Lefty," Babs called out angrily. "Your number sequences chew sunflower seeds!" She returned to George and Pat. "See what I mean?"

George nodded. "Could we see Lefty work out?" he asked Casey.

"Sure thing. Hey, 13! Take a few swings in the cage."

Steenbrenner, phone in hand, gestured to Lefty to get a bat.

On the mound there was a strange device with a mechanical arm. A player carrying a bucket of baseballs stood next to it, feeding it balls one at a time.

"That's a weird-looking pitcher," Pat joked.

George laughed. "It's an automatic pitching machine, Pat. Sort of like a robot."

Lefty was at the plate. The machine was switched

on. As fast as the machine could pitch, Lefty would hit the ball deep into the stands. Left field, right field, center field. Lefty hit both right-handed and left-handed. Pat and George watched in awe as 15 pitches in a row were drilled out of the park.

"That's the most incredible hitting I've ever seen," George said.

Casey smiled. "It took him a long time to come to this but then Rome wasn't built in a day and neither was Kalamazoo Michigan although it looks like it and I'm not the first one to say that neither because when Babe Ruth first came up to the bigs a lot of folks was saying, 'It's just for a cup of coffee,' but he showed everyone he was here for the whole enchilada with beef and extra salsa because he hit 714 runs in his career."

Pat stared at Casey. George, the baseball fan, added a postscript. "And he had very tiny feet, too."

Casey stared at George.

They were interrupted by Steenbrenner, who was calling out to some people scattered in the stands behind home plate. "What do you think of that?" he yelled up at them, pointing at Lefty.

"Who are those people, Babs?" Pat asked.

"Major league talent scouts. They're looking Lefty over."

"Let's see your boy pitch," someone called. Steenbrenner nodded to Lefty, who picked up his glove and walked to the mound.

George turned to Casey. "I used to be able to give that ball a ride when I was a youth."

Casey shrugged. "You want to step in against Number 13, it's okay with me."

George took off his jacket and handed it to Pat. She shook her head as she watched George pick up a bat, swing it three times, put it down and get another that he liked better.

Casey turned to Pat. "He's got a good swing for a mathematician and that's not something I say about everyone especially to someone who is almost a perfect stranger because I just met you a few minutes ago."

Pat smiled. "George never ceases to amaze me."

George stepped up to the plate. "Go ahead, Lefty!" he yelled. "Lemme see whatcha got on that old apple."

Lefty wound up and pitched the ball underhand so fast that no one saw it coming, especially George. The pitch thwacked into the catcher's mitt, its force propelling the catcher into a backward somersault.

"Throw it again," George called.

Lefty pitched again, in the same unusual underhand style. Again, the ball hit the glove before George could even lift the bat from his shoulder.

"Just hold your bat out and he'll hit it for you," Steenbrenner yelled.

George got into a bunting crouch and held the bat out over the plate. Lefty pitched again. There was a loud splitting sound as the ball slammed into the bat and broke it in two.

George was still shaking his head when he returned to Pat, Babs, and Casey. "That's the most outstanding pitching I've ever seen."

"Ever *not* seen," Pat corrected him.

George turned to Casey. "How fast does he throw the ball, Casey?"

"Faster than he used to I can tell you that and I

have."

Babs picked up something that looked like a hair dryer and said, "Let's find out exactly how fast."

"What's that, Babs?" Pat asked.

"It's a radar gun. It uses radio waves to calculate the speed of the baseball. It's like the guns police use to track speeders on the highway." Babs handed it to George. "Here, try it."

George aimed the gun at Lefty's next pitch and looked at the readout. "Must be something wrong with it." He shook the gun. "Nobody has ever thrown a baseball 134 miles per hour."

"We had the gun checked, Mr. Frankly," Babs said. "It's accurate."

Casey smiled. "And that was his change-up."

Lefty wound up for another pitch. George aimed the radar gun as the ball whizzed into the catcher's mitt. "Wow, 143 miles per hour!" George gasped. "The fastest anybody can throw in the big leagues is maybe 105, and then only once in a while."

Out on the field, Steenbrenner threw a warm-up jacket over Lefty's shoulders and said, "That's enough for today. Into the training room and I'll ice you down."

Lefty stared into space. "Isn't it a great day for baseball?" he asked in a flat voice. Then the two walked off together.

George watched them leave the field. "He's the most amazing player I've ever seen," he said.

Pat nodded agreement. "Thank you for letting us watch the workout, Casey."

"Sure thing any time at all except of course when I'm getting gasoline for my tractor or eating in a fancy

Italian restaurant."

As Casey walked away, Babs said to George and Pat, "Let's go check and see if Lefty put up a number sequence today."

The threesome headed down a long tunnel into the locker room. They walked down a line of lockers to one with a big number 13 on the front. A large padlock sealed the locker.

"No number sequence," said Babs sadly. "He usually tapes the envelope to his locker."

As they left the room, Babs switched off the lights. Suddenly, the three noticed something strange. In the darkness, there was a red glow pulsing around the edges of one locker.

It was locker number 13.

DUM DE DUM DUM

CHAPTER
3

When Pat walked in the door of Mathnet HQ the next morning, George was already on the phone. "No sense at all? Uh-huh. The numbers get larger and smaller again. What else? He repeats himself. Hmmmm. Maybe he's got a numerical stutter. Okay, Babs. We'll be in touch."

George hung up. "Morning, Pat."

"Morning, George. How's Babs?"

"She got a sequence from Lefty today, but it didn't make any more sense to her than the last few."

Benny came in, carrying a report, and greeted the Mathnetters. "Morning, each."

"I asked Benny to do a little sleuthing, Pat. Any luck, Benny?"

"Not much," Benny answered. "He did play some ball in college."

"Who?" Pat asked.

"Any good?" said George, ignoring Pat's question.

"Not much," Benny answered. "Pitched in a few games. Had an ERA of 9.75."

"Who?" Pat repeated.

"Was he a 'stick'?" George went on, again ignoring Pat.

"Couldn't hit his hat," Benny replied.

"Hey! Who???" Pat asked, her voice rising.

Both men looked straight at Pat this time. Then Benny turned back to George. "I thought you said she wasn't into baseball, George."

Pat took a deep breath. "Would you two mind sharing your gibberish with me?"

Benny smiled and sat down on the edge of Pat's desk. "George asked me to check out Dr. Frank N. Steenbrenner."

"Lefty's keeper?"

"Right," said Benny. "He played baseball at Michigan Agricultural College for a season and a half, then got kicked off the team. I couldn't find out why. I haven't been able to reach his old coach by phone, but here's his name and address." Benny handed a slip of paper to George.

"Earl 'Red' Koch, Red Cedar River, West Lansing, Michigan," George read. "Ever been to West Lansing, Michigan, Pat?"

"You mean you're going to fly to West Lansing?" Benny asked.

George said, "Nope, we can't."

Pat looked at him. "Why not?"

"It's too expensive. We're going by bus," George announced.

* * *

It was a long ride, but mercifully for Pat, she slept during most of George's rambling lecture on how to throw a slider. He also gave his sleeping partner some tips on disguising one's motion when throwing a change-up. By the time they reached West Lansing, Pat was awake and George had moved onto strategies against a left-handed pitcher.

Before you could say 'Jackie Robinson,' they were knocking on the door of the Koch residence. A woman answered. When she found out who they were, she introduced herself as Mrs. Koch.

"It's so nice of you to call on my husband," she said, "He's in his trophy room."

They found the coach, wearing a Michigan Agricultural College sweatshirt and baseball cap, with a whistle around his neck. He was sitting at a desk with absolutely nothing on it. Behind the desk were many trophy shelves, also empty.

George reached out to shake hands. "Coach Koch? I'm George Frankly and this is my partner, Pat—"

"Tuesday, Mathnet." Pat showed her Mathnet badge.

The coach looked at George's hand and shook Pat's badge. It was immediately clear to the detectives that Coach Koch's game was missing a few innings.

They all sat down, and George said, "Coach Koch, we came to ask you about a student athlete you used to coach."

"Are you sure it was me?" Koch asked.

George said, "Yes, sir. His name was Frank N. Steenbrenner. Does that name ring any bells? He was a pitcher."

"It doesn't ring any bells, but I remember him."

"Can you tell us about him?" Pat asked.

"Yes. His nickname was Cornfield, because when he pitched, the batter would knock the ball into the cornfield for a home run. He wasn't very good."

SPORTS
COBBS TO BE
SOLD TO HIGHEST
BIDDER,
MAN WITH GOLDEN
ARM TO BE AUCTIONED
FRIDAY.

"Is that why you kicked him off the team, Coach Koch?" asked George.

"Oh, no. No one on the team was any good. I kicked him off for betting on the games. He was very good at that. Made a fortune."

"Did he bet with the other players?" Pat asked.

"Oh, sure, and lots of other people, too. The athletic director, the president, me—"

George interrupted. "Coach Koch, do you remember what Steenbrenner majored in while he was in college?"

The coach thought for a minute, then said, "He changed his major several times, I remember that. He started out in hotel management, then switched to animal husbandry, then sports medicine for a time . . . then something else."

There was a pause, and George asked, "Do you remember what?"

"Not offhand."

Pat stood and said, "Well, Coach Koch, you've been a big help."

The coach shook his head. "I'm sorry."

George said, "If you think of what Steenbrenner got his degree in, let us know, will you, Coach Koch?"

The coach smiled. "I hope so."

* * *

When the detectives arrived back at Mathnet HQ after their trip, it was business as usual until Benny bounced through the door with a newspaper under his arm. "Hi, Mathnetters. How's tricks?"

"Hi, Benny," said Pat.

"What's new in the undercover cop business?" George asked.

"I don't know about the undercover business, but the sports world is abuzz." Benny handed the newspaper to George. "They're all talking about your buddy, Dr. Frank N. Steenbrenner."

"What about him?" Pat asked.

George opened the paper and read the headline aloud.

COBBS TO BE SOLD TO HIGHEST BIDDER
MAN WITH GOLDEN ARM TO BE AUCTIONED FRIDAY

Pat looked puzzled. "What does that mean?

Benny explained, "Steenbrenner is going to auction Lefty to a major league team with the bidding to start at 100 million dollars. It seems crazy to spend millions for an over-the-hill pitcher who happens to be on a hot streak, but baseball is a crazy business. All 28 teams are interested."

"But how can he do that? Doesn't Casey Bengal have Lefty under contract?" Pat asked.

Benny shook his head. "Casey didn't bother. He figured Lefty would never amount to anything again."

"According to the paper," George added, "by the time the Rowdies realized they had a hot property on their hands, Steenbrenner had already signed Lefty to a personal services contract."

"This is terrible," said Pat. "If the Rowdies lose Lefty now, it will break Babs's heart—not to mention Casey's."

"I know," said George. "And Casey has a good shot at managing in the big leagues if the Rowdies win the minor league World Series. Without Lefty, they won't stand a chance."

"You know," said Benny, "the auction isn't until Friday, and there is one more game on Thursday. If they win that, the Rowdies at least clinch the pennant."

"But they'll get creamed in the series without him," George said.

"You can't be too sure, George," said Benny.

"What do you mean?" asked Pat.

Benny took a deep breath. "Adversity often brings out the best in people. You know, the underdog rises up to smite the favorite. The team rallies and finds that they're not just a collection of individuals, but a close-knit, well-oiled organization. When the odds are against them, they stand tall and lash out, withering their opponents and crushing them into a helpless, worthless pile of gelatinous gunk."

Pat and George gaped at Benny in awe.

"Benny, what a moving statement," Pat managed to say, a catch in her voice.

George asked, "Benny, do you really think the Rowdies can do it without Lefty?"

"Not in a million years!"

DUM DE DUM DUM

CHAPTER

4

Thursday morning Pat made her way through the commuting crowds to the relative peace and quiet of Mathnet. It was quieter than usual. When she entered the office, her partner seemed in a daze. His glazed eyes moved back and forth between the number sequence on the board and the yellow pad he was writing on.

"Morning, George."

"Morning, Martha."

"Martha? Martha's your wife. George, did you sleep last night?"

"Not really. I've had Lefty's last number sequence in my head, and I can't get rid of it."

George's eyes began to close. Pat stared at him, smiled, and shook her head. The phone rang.

George said, "Just five more minutes, Martha . . ."

Pat answered. "Mathnet, Tuesday. Oh, hi, Babs. What? Where? We'll be right there." She put the phone down and gave George a gentle shake. "Babs has Lefty with her and wants to meet us. Let's roll."

George stumbled to his feet, stuffed his notes in his briefcase, and said, "Let's what?"

While George napped, Pat drove the NYPD car to a restaurant near the Rowdies' stadium, where Babs and

Lefty awaited their arrival. The brisk air and the anticipation of having an opportunity to talk with Lefty shook George from his daze. They spotted Babs and made their way to her table.

Babs jumped up and welcomed them. "Thanks for coming. Lefty, these are my friends—"

They shook hands. "Pat Tuesday."

"George Frankly, Mathnet."

As George sat down, he asked, "Babs, how did you get Lefty away from Dr. Steenbrenner?"

"Steenbrenner was on the phone talking to some major league owner, so I called you and then asked Lefty to come out for a soda. I thought you could help me change Lefty's mind about leaving the Rowdies. But it's okay. I've already convinced him to call off the auction."

Lefty had a blank look on his face as he said woodenly, "Yes. She has convinced me to call off the auction."

George smiled. "Terrific. That means you'll stay with the Rowdies through the season."

"And we'll win the pennant and then go on to the World Series," Babs added happily.

Babs's smile faded and her eyes widened as she looked across the restaurant. George and Pat looked up to see a red-faced man storming toward their table. Pat stood up. "What do you want, Dr. Frank N. Steenbrenner?"

"*My* property. Get up, Lefty. Now!" He grabbed Lefty by the ear.

Babs jumped to her feet. "Dr. Steenbrenner, I just want you to know that Lefty has agreed to stay with the team through the World Series."

Steenbrenner growled, "He hasn't agreed to anything. I hold his contract, and it's being sold tomorrow morning. His word means nothing. Nothing, do you hear me?"

As Steenbrenner led Lefty away, Babs called out, "And another thing—where's my number sequence?"

Walking out the door, Steenbrenner yelled back, "You'll get it, you little baby!"

Babs sat down, close to tears. "Sorry for dragging you all the way out here for nothing."

"That's okay," George said, patting her arm. "We tried."

Babs got up and put on her River Vale Rowdies jacket. "I've gotta go. The big game starts soon."

"We'll come and watch," said Pat.

Babs smiled. "Great. I'll get you a couple of ducats."

Pat looked at George. "A couple of what?"

"Two freebies for the game."

Pat took George's arm. "Pard, take me out to the ball game."

* * *

Pat and George made their way into the rapidly filling stadium and found their seats. They had to dodge around other fans, hot dog and soft drink vendors, and foul balls being drilled into the stands as the teams took batting practice. The sights, the sounds, and the smells were wonderful; and the Mathnetters were looking forward to an exciting couple of hours at the old ball game. Their seats were behind first base, so they had a perfect view of the diamond. George bought a box of popcorn, which he hugged to his chest as they squeezed past other fans. He plopped down on the bleacher.

"Hey," said the man next to him. "You're sitting on my hot dog, Mac!"

George got up slowly. Sure enough, there was a squished wiener, complete with mustard and relish, on the seat. "Here you go, buddy," George said, handing the mess to his neighbor.

The fan looked at it, then at George. "It's all flat!" he exclaimed.

George examined the flat hot dog. "Yes, sir, but if you will note, the volume has not changed, only the shape. You will obtain the same nutrients as though I had never sat on it."

"George, look," Pat interrupted. "It's Babs. Over by the dugout. She's motioning for us to come sit down."

George and Pat got up to go. As he edged his way past the unhappy hot dog owner, George stumbled and spilled the man's popcorn.

The fan looked up at George. "Will you be coming back?" he asked slowly.

George shrugged. "I think so."

The man got up, brushed popcorn off his pants, and ran for the nearest exit.

"Goodness," said George, "I wonder where he's off to."

Pat and George headed to the dugout. Babs was waiting for them with an envelope in her hand.

"I got another number sequence from Lefty, but I haven't had a chance to look at it, what with the big game and all. Maybe you could—?"

"Sure thing," Pat said. "Come back to the office with us and we'll work on it."

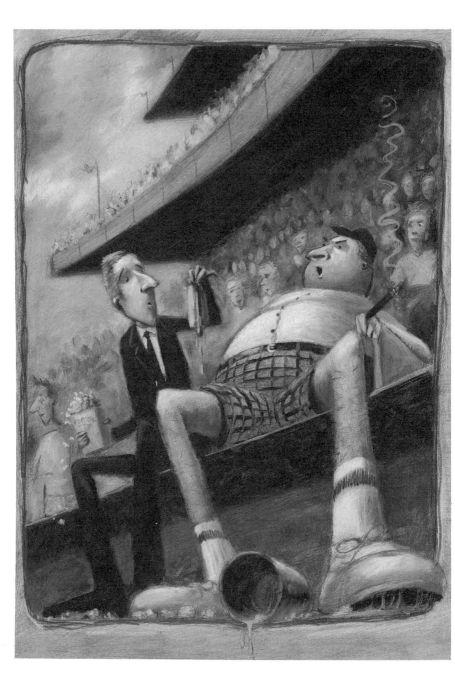

"What about the game?" George cried. Pat poked him with her elbow. "I mean, let's go back to the office right away and work on it."

Babs smiled. "Thanks, Mr. Frankly." She looked back at the field. "I can miss the first few innings."

* * *

When they got back to Mathnet HQ, George wrote Lefty's newest "answer" on the blackboard. It was just as odd as the last one.

As she stared at the numbers, Pat had an idea. "Babs, did you and Lefty ever use alphanumeric codes?"

"What's alphanumeric?"

George answered. "It's where you let numbers stand for letters so you can write coded messages. 1=A, 2=B, 3=C, and so forth."

"Yes, we did that for a while—birthday cards, notes, stuff like that. But then we got into the sequence game, which is more fun."

"But take a look at this sequence again," Pat suggested. "Could it be an alphanumeric message?"

"Cool," said Babs. "I never even thought of that. We haven't sent codes in such a long time."

"Let's go back and look at the first message," said George. "It's shorter." He dug through his briefcase and found Lefty's first sequence answer.

He wrote it on the board.

3-1-16-20-9-22-5

First they tried the simplest code, using 1 as a stand-in for A and on up to 26 for Z. Using that code, they discovered that the sequence spelled out the word *captive*.

A=1	F=6	K=11	P=16	U=21
B=2	G=7	L=12	Q=17	V=22
C=3	H=8	M=13	R=18	W=23
D=4	I=9	N=14	S=19	X=24
E=5	J=10	O=15	T=20	Y=25
				Z=26

3	1	16	20	9	22	5
C	A	P	T	I	V	E

"Maybe Lefty is in trouble," said Babs with a frown. "He went back to the old code to tell me."

Next, they turned their attention to Lefty's latest message.

11-9-4-14-1-16-16-5-4-313-23-98-114-10025

"I'll be hornswoggled," George said.

Pat stared at her partner and asked, "What is it, George?"

"That's the same message he sent the other day."

"It is?"

George checked it out. "Exactly the same."

The Mathnetters began the decoding process. Babs looked at her watch and gasped. She ran to the door. "I've got to get back to the game," she said.

"Benny will drive you to the stadium," offered Pat. "Hurry!"

George was still standing by the board. "Look at this, Pat. Using the same code as before, 11 is K, 9 is I, 4 is D . . . Holy cow!"

Pat nearly fell off her chair. "What? What?"

"Sorry," George said, "but . . . the ball game! . . . I wonder how Lefty is doing. Keep working on that code, Pat."

Pat sighed and moved to the blackboard as George turned on the television. He watched with rapt attention as the award-seeking sportscasters Dick and Vern gave their play-by-play coverage of the championship game between the River Vale Rowdies and the Secaucus Seven.

"No score after eight and a half innings. Have you ever seen a game like this in your life, Vern?"

"No, Dick. But then, I'm very nearsighted."

"Strike three! We're in the bottom of the ninth inning, two out, and Lefty Cobbs, who is pitching a perfect game, is coming up to bat."

"He's faced 27 batters and hasn't allowed a single hit, Dick."

Pat was busy trying to decode the message when George turned to update her on the game. "Did you hear that, Pat? Two out in the last of the ninth, no score, and Lefty's at bat."

"George, I think I'm getting a very strange message."

George didn't hear her. He had turned back to the baseball game.

"Here's the first pitch. Low and away for ball one."

"He couldn't have hit that ball with a boat oar."

"Ball two!"

Pat had made some progress with her decoding. "George?"

"Not now, Pat. The game is on the line."

The television blared. "Ball three, in the dirt. And here's the three-and-0 pitch to Lefty Cobbs." There was the crack of the bat and a loud cheer from the fans. "That ball could be out of here . . . away back into left center field. . . . Home run! The Rowdies win it, the Rowdies win it, the Rowdies—"

"George!"

George turned off the television set, and turned to Pat with a smile. "Did you see that? Lefty just won the game and the pennant."

"George, listen to me. Lefty's been kidnapped!"

DUM DE DUM DUM

CHAPTER

5

George stared at his partner for a minute. Then he smiled. "Well, for someone who is kidnapped, he sure has a good stroke."

Pat had lost her patience. She grabbed George by the shoulders and spun him to face the blackboard. "George, look at this!"

George read:

```
11 - 9 - 4 - 14 - 1 - 16 - 16 - 5 - 4
 K   I   D   N    A   P    P    E   D

313  - 23  - 98  - 114  - 10025
CAC    W      IH     AAD     AOOBE
```

"'Kidnapped cac w'. . . . It makes no sense, Pat."

"The first part does."

"Pat, it's some kind of joke Lefty is playing on Babs. He's not kidnapped. I just saw him win one of the most dramatic games in the history of baseball."

"I know it doesn't seem to make sense, George, but . . ." Their conversation was interrupted by the intercom buzzer. Pat answered. "Tuesday. Yes, Sergeant Abruzzi. Who? Oh! Send him in."

George looked at Pat expectantly, but before she could answer, the door opened and Coach Earl Koch walked in.

"Coach Koch," George said. "What a surprise."

The coach took off his hat and twisted it in his hands as he looked at his shoes. "I hope I'm not intruding on you."

"Not at all," Pat said. "What can we do for you?"

Coach Koch brightened. "I remembered the answer to that question you asked me the other day. You know, about Frank N. Steenbrenner and what his degree was in."

"Yes, Coach Koch. What was his major?"

"Robotics."

The coach definitely had gotten the Mathnetters' attention.

"Robotics?" George was amazed.

Proudly the coach said, "Yep. I looked it up."

George shook their visitor's hand. "Thanks. That was very nice of you, Coach Koch. But why did you come all the way from West Lansing to New York just to tell us that? Why didn't you just call us on the phone?"

The coach, pausing on his way out the door, asked, "The what?"

Pat and George looked at each other. George broke the silence. "Never mind. Bye, Coach." He turned to Pat. "What do you think, Pard?"

Pat looked at the partially decoded message on the board. "George, I still think Lefty has been kidnapped."

* * *

At Mathnet HQ the next morning, Pat was still puzzling over the rest of the code when George came in, stuffing some food in his mouth. Pat looked closer.

"George, are you eating pizza for breakfast?"

"Uh-huh. I bought it downstairs."

"Yuck!"

"It was on sale. Day old." He put his briefcase down and looked over at Pat. This morning she was the one who looked dazed. "Are you still working on that code, Pard? I tell you, it's some kind of joke Lefty's playing."

"I don't think so."

George looked at the board. "Well, are you having any luck?"

"No, and I've been at it all night, too."

"Staying up all night is not good for you, Pat. You need your beauty sleep."

As George walked over to the board, Pat glared at him. He didn't seem to notice.

George just said, "What were you trying?"

"I thought maybe Lefty changed the code in the middle. You know, maybe he started at a different letter, 1 stands for B, 2 stands for C—"

"Doesn't work?" George asked.

"No, I've tried everything I can think of, George." Pat walked across the room and slumped in her desk chair. She cushioned her head in her hands and mumbled, "Maybe it is just a joke. But then there's this thing about Steenbrenner—"

"Majoring in robotics? What does that have to do with Lefty? Anyway, a lot of people major in strange things in college. This one guy I knew studied owls."

"Who?" Pat asked.

Just then, the door burst open and Babs rushed in.

George and Pat gave her a big hug.

"What a great game," said George, "Lefty looked phenomenal, Babs."

"He also looked strange, but that's been true ever since he hooked up with Dr. Steenbrenner. Did you guys have any luck with his message?"

"Not much, Babs," said George, "and Pat's been working on it all night."

Babs looked at the board. "'Kidnapped'! And 'cac' . . . what does that mean?"

"We don't know," George said, "I think it's a joke. It's pretty obvious from what we saw last night that Lefty hasn't been kidnapped."

Babs was worried. "But what if he *has* been kidnapped?"

"Then who won that game for the Rowdies?" George asked.

But Babs wasn't paying attention to him. "If Lefty was really kidnapped," she said, "what kind of message would he send?"

"He might try to tell us where he's being held captive," said Pat.

Babs walked over to the board and pointed to the message. "What if this gibberish isn't letters but numbers, like in an address?"

Pat snapped her fingers. "That's it, Babs! One thing that jumped out at me earlier was the last five numbers."

Babs pointed. "1-0-0-2-5?"

"Yes," Pat said. "It just happens to be a New York City zip code. I have a friend who lives in that area. George, please get our zip code directory so that we can check out Babs's theory."

Pat and Babs looked back at the board. "We can forget about these first nine numbers," Babs said.

"Right. They spell 'kidnapped.'"

"And the last five, because they're the zip code."

"We don't know that yet, Babs," Pat cautioned. "That's our hypothesis."

"Yes, but it's a pretty good guess if you ask me." George opened up a map of New York City zip codes.

"The 10025 zip code is in the Upper West Side of Manhattan," he pointed out. "It covers the area from 92nd Street to 114th Street."

"How about east and west boundaries, George?"

"Central Park bounds the east and the Hudson River the west. The address numbers run from 2 to about 325."

Babs thought for a minute. "Our next set of numbers is 313, then a space and 23. I've got it! Lefty is at 313 23rd Street."

"N.G., Babs," George said.

"N.G.?"

Pat explained George's shorthand. "N.G. means no good."

"Why?"

"There's no 23rd Street in that area," George said.

Babs tried again. "Maybe it's 313-23-98 114th Street. There's a 114th Street."

"Yes, but not with those kinds of numbers," Pat pointed out.

George said, "We're forgetting something. New York is divided east and west by Fifth Avenue. The zip code 10025 is on the West Side. The word *West* should be a part of the address."

Mathnet HQ was silent as the threesome stared at

the sequence. Babs pointed to a number. "Isn't 23 the number for the letter W in our alphanumeric code?"

"Brilliant thought, Babs," Pat said. "Maybe Lefty was mixing letters and numbers in with the code, to give us a street address."

"So, it could be 313 West 98th Street."

"Could be, George. I'll go get the map and we'll see what's there."

Babs said to George, "But Mr. Frankly, we have 3 numbers left over." She pointed with the chalk at the numbers 1, 1, 4.

```
313 - 23 - 98 - 114 - 10025
#313   W.  98ᵀᴴST.   ?   10025
```

"There's no letter in the alphabet that corresponds to 114," she added.

"Nope. Sure isn't."

Pat returned with a map. "There's an apartment building at 313 West 98th. It's a big one, with about 80 apartments."

"Maybe 114 is the apartment number!" Babs said.

"Could be, Babs. Shall we check it out, Pard?" George asked.

"What if we're wrong, George?"

"I don't know. I guess we'll feel silly." George opened the door. "You get Benny and his cab. I'll get a search warrant."

DUM DE DUM DUM

CHAPTER

6

Benny's undercover Checker cab was waiting in front of NYPD Headquarters a half-hour later. Pat and Babs waited several more minutes until George appeared, search warrant in hand. The traffic was heavy as Benny slithered through side streets to the West Side. Benny, a New York driver, complained about New York drivers all the way up to West 98th Street. He double-parked in front of Number 313.

They entered the foyer and rushed to the buzzer panel that listed the apartments by number and name.

Pat ran her finger up and down, checking the numbers. "There's no apartment 114. They're all numbered by the floor and a letter."

There was a pause as they looked at each other and heaved a sigh of defeat. "Well, at least we tried," Babs said. They turned toward the door.

Suddenly Babs stopped. "Wait! If 4 stands for D in our code, maybe 114 is—"

They turned back to the panel and said in unison, "11 D."

Babs found it first. "Look," she said.

"Just what I expected," said George. Next to the buzzer for apartment 11 D was the name of its occupant—Dr. Frank N. Steenbrenner. Benny checked his police revolver as the elevator creaked very slowly from the lobby to the eleventh floor. In front of 11 D, Benny gestured for Babs, Pat, and George to move out of harm's way. He rang the bell.

After a moment, a gruff voice answered. "Yeah. Who is it?"

Benny answered in a high voice. "It's Little Red Riding Hood. I've come with a basket of goodies for Grandma."

The door opened a crack. In a lightning move, Benny pushed the door wide open. The man on the other side, a mean-looking thug holding a .38 Special, looked surprised, to say the least.

Benny grabbed the man's gun and said, "A basket of goodies and a search warrant. Mind if we come in?"

Babs ran past them calling, "Lefty? Are you here?"

Pat and George followed. They found Lefty, bound and gagged, in the bedroom. Babs took off the gag. Pat and George worked on the ropes.

"Lefty! Is it really you?"

"Yes, Babs, it's really me."

They hugged. George pointed to the thug. "And who might this be?"

Lefty rubbed his chafed wrists. "He's my 'baby-sitter.' He and Steenbrenner have held me prisoner here for the last six weeks."

"If you've been a prisoner, who's been posing as number 13?" Pat asked.

"You may find this hard to believe, but it's an android," Lefty explained. "He's a robot, an artificially created man." It was then that George and Pat noticed the artificial arms, legs, feet and other body parts strewn about the place.

"Do you know where Steenbrenner is now, Lefty?"

George asked. "We've got to find him."

"I heard him say they were going to the locker room to pick up a few things and then he was going to—"

"The auction!" George shouted. "Holy smokes! We've got to stop him before he makes a mockery of our national pastime. Come on."

* * *

Everyone squeezed into Benny's cab and headed for the hotel where the auction was being held. On the way, Lefty explained that Steenbrenner had been hanging around the Rowdies for some time. When Lefty got the flu six weeks ago, he assumed Steenbrenner was a medical doctor and went to him for help. Once inside the apartment, he became a prisoner while Steenbrenner used him as the model for the android.

"Steenbrenner felt humiliated when he failed at baseball," Lefty said. "He studied robotics just so he could get revenge. He thought he could both ruin baseball and make himself a fortune. He was just waiting for the right time and the right person. I guess I was it."

Lefty's only hope was to get a message to Babs. "I convinced Steenbrenner that Babs would get suspicious if she didn't get any sequences," he told the others. "He let me work out some codes. Then he left them on my locker for Babs to find."

The cab pulled up to the hotel. Inside, Pat spotted a sign in front of a pair of double doors. It read Baseball Auction. When they all got closer, the others couldn't

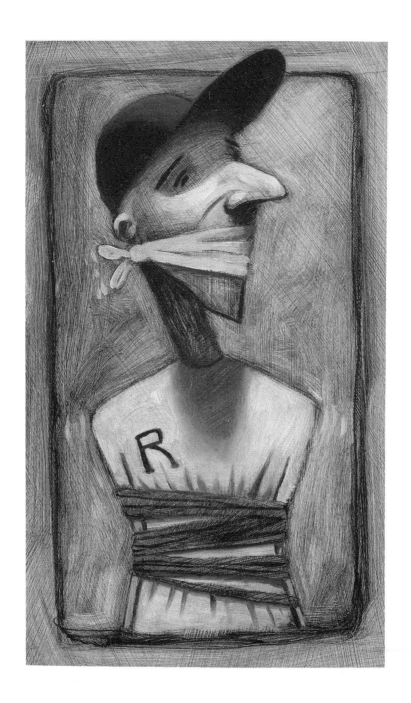

help staring at Lefty, because they could hear his voice coming from the other side of the doors. It was an eerie sensation.

"Today, I consider myself the luckiest man on the face of the earth," the android Lefty was saying. "My years with the Rowdies have been grand..."

As the droning went on, the Mathnetters instructed Babs and Lefty to stay put. The detectives entered the crowded room to confront Steenbrenner. The evil doctor was standing near the dais, where the android continued to bore the onlookers. "The game is over, Steenbrenner," George said loudly.

Steenbrenner grinned. "You're right, Mr. Frankly. The game is over." He showed George and Pat a check. "Lefty Cobbs has just been sold to the Chicago Cubs for 313 million dollars."

Pat said, "Wait until we tell the Cubs they own an android, not a real player."

"Please!" Steenbrenner replied. "Are you trying to tell these intelligent people that Lefty is some kind of robot? Ha! My money and I are leaving."

He headed for the door. George rushed to intercept him, accidentally tripping a passing waiter. The waiter's tray tilted, and a water glass slid off the tray. Before anyone could catch the glass, the water doused the android Lefty. Sparks and smoke filled the air. Everyone in the room gasped in shock.

"... and maaake thiiisss theee finneeestt gammme of baaasseeballll innnn hissssttttoooorrrreeeeeeee," the android hissed, sparks shooting from its mouth. Then it collapsed on the dais with a loud crash.

Pat went up to the dais as Benny grabbed Steenbrenner. "Ladies and gentlemen," she said, pointing down to the android, "this is not Lefty Cobbs. This was a fraud." She pointed to the door. "There is the real Lefty Cobbs."

The people in the crowd greeted Lefty and Babs with thunderous applause.

Casey Bengal joined the group as Benny led Steenbrenner away. "Wait a minute or even longer if you can but explain to me one thing. You ain't twins are you 13?"

Lefty laughed and said, "No, Casey, I'm not twins."

Casey patted Lefty on the back. "Good 13 cause if you were I'd have to change your name to 26."

* * *

Lefty and Babs thanked everyone for their help then left with Casey for the first game of the minor league World Series. Lefty was scheduled to start. The Mathnetters wished them luck and returned to HQ.

George picked up a file folder that had been placed on his desk and looked through it. "So that's how he did it."

"What, George?" asked Pat.

"This is a report from the lab. That glow in Lefty's locker was from a device used to recharge batteries. When Steenbrenner pretended to take the android Lefty into the dugout to ice him down, he was actually recharging the batteries."

"But how did he control it?"

"With his cordless telephone. He had a code set up. If he wanted a fastball, he'd push one button. A curve was another button, and so on. The android could have struck out every batter it faced, but that might have raised a few eyebrows."

Pat nodded. "So Steenbrenner had to give up a few hits, a few runs, just to make it look legitimate."

"Right, Pat. With batting, he didn't know what the pitcher was going to throw. So he couldn't control where the ball would go. Once in a while, someone would catch the ball and the fake Lefty would be out."

"Well, that almost wraps it up, Pard. Except I wonder how the minor league World Series is going."

"Me too."

The phone rang. "I'll get it. Mathnet, Frankly. Oh, hi, Babs."

Pat picked up her extension. "Hi, Babs. How's the game going?"

"Well, Mathnetters, there's good news and there's bad news."

George asked, "What's the bad news, Babs?"

"It's the bottom of the first inning, the score is 9–zip against us, the other guys have batted around, and Casey just yanked Lefty."

"Sorry about that, Babs," said Pat. "What's the good news?"

"Lefty's back!"

DUM DE DUM DUM

EPILOGUE

Frank N. Steenbrenner was tried and convicted in Manhattan in and for the City of New York and the government of the United States. He was convicted of a 180.51, tampering with a sports contest in the first degree; a 245.05, offensive exhibition; and a 190.65, scheme to defraud. He was put away for the rest of his natural life. Roy 'Lefty' Cobbs, the android, was reassembled and is currently hosting a network newscast.

ACTIVITIES

SLUGGING SLUGGERS

The box below shows batting data for Roy Lefty Cobbs's teammates on the River Vale Rowdies. Compute the slugging averages for each player for five games. AB is the number of times the player is at bat. 1B, 2B, 3B and HR are the number of singles, doubles, triples and home runs hit. A home run counts for four bases. Divide the total number of bases by the number of times at bat to find the slugging average.

RIVER VALE ROWDIES — FIVE-GAME TOTAL

PLAYER	AB At Bat	1B Singles	2B Doubles	3B Triples	HR Home Run	Total Bases	SLUGGING AVERAGE
31 Hern Andez	16	4	2	0	1		
25 Yo-yo Bear	17	2	0	0	2		
7 Earl Extremeski	17	4	0	0	0		
82 Lou Ferring	18	1	1	0	0		
26 Moe D. Gaggio	19	3	0	0	0		
34 Dodger Hairless	21	3	1	0	0		
72 Robin Jackson	15	1	0	0	0		
48 William Teds	15	2	0	0	1		

1. Which player has the highest slugging average?____

2. Which player has the lowest slugging average?_____

3. If William Teds was at bat 15 times and got only 2 singles and 1 triple and never walked, how many times was he "out"?_____

GUESS MY RULE

Babs and Lefty try to stump each other when they play "Guess My Rule." Can you guess the next number(s) in these sequences they sent each other? Looking at differences between the numbers often helps.

    1) 1, 4, 7, 10, 13, ___, ___, ___, ___.

    2) 1, 3, 6, 10, 15, ___, ___, ___, ___.

    3) 2, 6, 12, 20, 30, ___, ___, ___, ___.

    4) 4, 7, 12, 19, 28, ___, ___, ___, ___.

    5) 5, 9, 17, 29, 45, ___, ___, ___, ___.

    6) 1, 2, 4, 8, 16, ___, ___, ___, ___.

    7) 3, 7, 16, 32, 57, ___, ___, ___, ___.

Sometimes Babs and Lefty drop the rule that says the numbers in a sequence must get bigger. Then the sequences can get pretty tricky!

    8) 9, 11, 8, 10, 7, 9, ___, ___, ___, ___.

    9) 20, 24, 14, 19, 10, 16, 8, ___, ___, ___, ___.

    10) 1, 1, 2, 3, 5, 8, 13, 21, ___, ___, ___, ___.

ALPHA NUMERIC CODES AND BASEBALL FACTS

Answer the questions. Then decode the answers. In the code, 1 stands for the letter "A," 2 stands for "B," 3 stands for "C,"... and 26 stands for "Z." For numbers greater than 26, recycle through the alphabet. So, for example, 27 also stands for "A," 28 stands for "B," 29 stands for "C" and so on.

1. Who invented the game of baseball?

    1 - 2 - 14 - 5 - 18

    4 - 15 - 21 - 2 - 12 - 5 - 4 - 27 - 25

2. Who holds the record for the most home runs?

    8 - 53 - 40 - 11   27 - 1 - 44 - 15 - 66

3. In which U.S. city and state was the first World Series played?

    54 - 15 - 45 - 20 - 15 - 66

   39 - 53 - 19 - 71 - 27 - 3 - 60 - 21 - 45 - 5 - 20 - 72 - 45

4. In which U.S. city and state was the first baseball game played?

    40 - 31 - 23   25 - 15 - 70 - 11

    14 - 5 - 75   51 - 41 - 18 - 63

5. Which baseball player has the most career hits?

    42 - 5 - 20 - 57   44 - 15 - 19 - 31

6. Where was the first World Series played outside of the U.S.?

    20 - 15 - 70 - 67 - 14 - 72 - 41

    29 - 53 - 14 - 1 - 30 - 27

7. Which baseball field was the last to have night games?

    23 - 18 - 9 - 33 - 12 - 57 - 77   6 - 35 - 57 - 12 - 4

ANSWERS

SLUGGING SLUGGERS:

Hern Andez	Total Bases: 12;	Slugging Average: .750
Yo-yo Bear	Total Bases: 10;	Slugging Average: .588
Earl Extremeski	Total Bases: 4;	Slugging Average: .235
Lou Ferring	Total Bases: 3;	Slugging Average: .167
Moe D. Gaggio	Total Bases: 3;	Slugging Average: .158
Dodger Hairless	Total Bases: 5;	Slugging Average: .238
Robin Jackson	Total Bases: 1;	Slugging Average: .067
William Teds	Total Bases: 6;	Slugging Average: .400

1) 31   2) 72   3) 12

GUESS MY RULE:

1) 16, 19, 22, 25
2) 21, 28, 36, 45
3) 42, 56, 72, 90
4) 39, 52, 67, 84
5) 65, 89, 117, 149
6) 32, 64, 128, 256
7) 93, 142, 206, 287
8) 6, 8, 5, 7
9) 15, 8, 16, 10
10) 34, 55, 89, 144

ALPHA-NUMERIC CODES AND BASEBALL FACTS

1) ABNER DOUBLEDAY
2) HANK AARON
3) BOSTON, MASSACHUSETTS
4) NEW YORK, NEW YORK
5) PETE ROSE
6) TORONTO, CANADA
7) WRIGLEY FIELD